Buffy the Barn Owl

With thanks to Julie and Gary Higgins for their help.

For a free color catalog describing Gareth Stevens' list of high-quality children's books call 1 (800) 433-0942

Library of Congress Cataloging-in-Publication Data

Burton, Jane.
  Buffy the barn owl / by Jane Burton; photography by Jane Burton
and Kim Taylor. — North American ed.
        p.   cm. — (Baby animals growing up)
  Includes index.
  Summary: Depicts a barn owl feeding, growing, and learning to hunt
and fly during the first year of its life.
  ISBN 0-8368-0202-0
    1. Barn owl—Development—Juvenile literature. [1. Barn owl.
2. Owls. 3. Animals—Infancy.] I. Taylor, Kim, ill. II. Title.
III. Series: Burton, Jane. Baby animals growing up.
  QL696.S85B86   1989
  598'.97—dc20   89-11410

This North American edition first published in 1989 by

Gareth Stevens Children's Books
7317 W. Green Tree Road
Milwaukee, Wisconsin 53223, USA

Format © 1989 by Gareth Stevens, Inc. Supplementary text © 1989 by
Gareth Stevens, Inc. Original text and photographs © 1988 by Jane Burton.
First published in Great Britain in 1988 by Macdonald & Co. Ltd.

Editors: Patricia Lantier and Rhoda Irene Sherwood
Cover design: Kate Kriege

Printed in the United States of America

1 2 3 4 5 6 7 8 9 95 94 93 92 91 90 89

Baby
Animals
Growing
Up!

Buffy the Barn Owl

JANE BURTON

Gareth Stevens Children's Books

MILWAUKEE

Wild barn owls are nesting in an old barn.
The mother sits on the eggs the whole time,
while the father brings mice for her to eat.

The owls have eight eggs. If all eight hatch, the owls will not be able to catch enough mice to feed the chicks. So four of the eggs are chosen to hatch in a warm box called an incubator.

Buffy, the first of them, has begun to hatch already. She has made a hole in the shell with her beak.

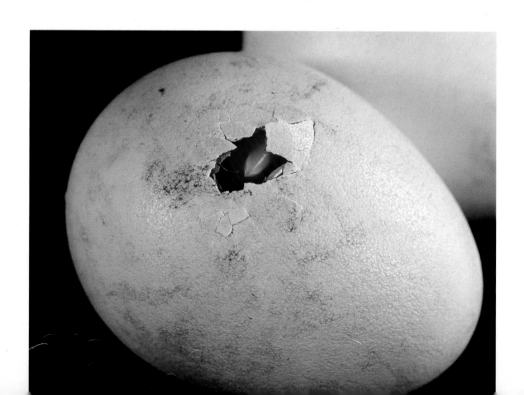

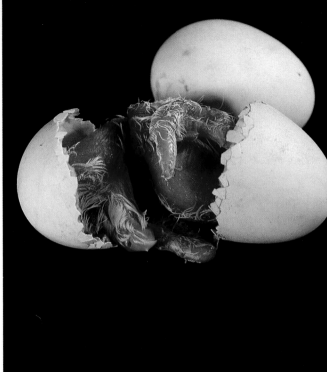

Buffy takes a long time to hatch. It has been two days since she made that first hole. Now she is quickly making a lot more holes. She turns inside the egg so that the small holes join to make one big slit. The holes cut the shell nearly all around. Buffy's wing pokes out.

At last the eggshell is held together by just a small piece of shell. Now Buffy heaves and pushes. Suddenly the two halves burst apart. Buffy kicks and scrambles free.

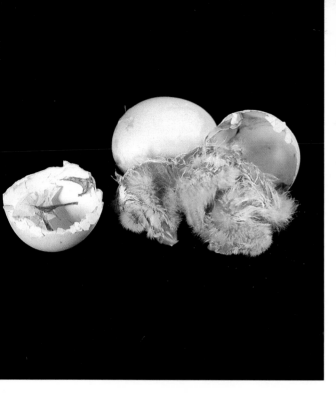

A newborn baby barn owl is not like a baby chick or a duckling. It is pink and blind and helpless. A chick or duckling is fluffy and can stand up and walk soon after hatching. Its eyes are wide open. But it will be days before Buffy can even sit up. It will be weeks before she can see.

Barn owl eggs do not hatch all at the same time. Buffy is two days old when Puff hatches. They sleep curled up together. Polly hatches five days after Puff and Humpty hatches three days later.

Five days old

Buffy and her sisters stay in their warm bed except for weighing time. Meals come four times a day. When Buffy is hungry she twitters. She is fed in a margarine tub, her head propped over the rim.

Buffy pecks tiny morsels of soft meat from a pair of tweezers. She cannot see the food. But when the tip of the tweezers touches her beak, she opens her mouth. The tweezers are like a mother owl's beak, feeding Buffy.

At first Buffy only eats a tiny amount, but as she gets bigger she can eat more. Weighing her each day determines if she is eating enough and growing fast.

Eight days old

Buffy is so big already that only her head would fit inside an egg now. She can sit up. She gives a great yawn, then settles down to sleep again. Sometimes she sleeps on her tummy. Sometimes she goes to sleep on her back with her feet in the air. She looks dead, until her wings twitch and she twitters in her sleep. She must be dreaming that she is flying!

Twelve days old

When Buffy wants to shift to a warmer spot, she shuffles along on her bottom. Or she can half-stand and stump about, like a little bent old person. She feels the way with her beak.

11

Fifteen days old

Buffy's eyes are slitting open at last. She sits in her feeding tub after a huge meal. Her tummy is as round and tight as a tennis ball. It emits alarming tummy rumbles. She shakes and shivers so the whole tub vibrates. She must go back into the warm cage to digest her meal.

Buffy and her three sisters live in a nursery cage now, heated by a heat lamp. To warm up after dinner, they crowd together under the lamp. Their first feathers, called "down," are too sparse to keep them warm yet.

Sixteen days old

Three in a boat and one overboard! Puff and Polly and Buffy can just fit in the tub, but there's no room for Humpty. All the owlets are hungry again and clamoring for food. They search about with their beaks. When Buffy and Humpty touch beaks, each one thinks that the other is going to feed her. They jab and bite each other's beak until Humpty topples backward.

After their meal, it is weighing time again. Buffy tests a weight with her beak.

Twenty-six days old

Buffy has sprouted a second coat of down. Now all fluffy and white, she *almost* looks pretty. At meal-times, there is only room in the tub for the two smallest owls who still need rather dainty bits of chopped meat to eat. Buffy is so big that she can gulp down a whole dead mouse at once. But she has some difficulty swallowing its tail. She looks a little uncomfortable, but such a big meal keeps her quiet for a long time.

Thirty days old

The owlets have grown so much that now, when they cluster under the lamp, they hit their heads on it if they're not careful.

Cream Cracker is just at that exploring and getting-into-everything stage. Now she has gotten into the barn owl nursery.

Buffy and Cream Cracker are the same age. They look the same size. But the kitten is heavier than Buffy. If they would sit still for a moment, they could be weighed!

Thirty-two days old

Every day Buffy swallows four mice whole. She digests the meaty parts, but not the hard bits. All the mouse bones and fur form a neat parcel, or pellet, inside her.

While Buffy is waiting to bring up a pellet, she looks sick. Then she just opens her mouth, out pops the pellet, and she is hungry again.

Thirty-eight days old

Buff-colored feathers have been sprouting all this time underneath Buffy's baby down. Now her wing feathers appear among the fluff. Short facial feathers form a disk. She begins to look more like a barn owl than a cuddly toy. She stands sturdily on spread toes, and she can run and climb, but she cannot fly yet.

Two months old

All the owlets can help themselves to their food now, even Humpty. She is still downy, but Buffy has lost most of her down. Puff and Polly still have fluffy skirts and knickers on. Little puffs of molted white down drift everywhere.

The four owlets live in the hay barn. They may still look cute, but they are *not* pets. They are growing up into dangerous birds of prey. Soon they will learn to catch mice for themselves.

21

Three months old

Buffy is beautiful now that she has lost her down. But she is fierce — like a wild owl.

All four owls can fly but not well yet. They practice flying to strengthen their wing muscles. Buffy whirrs her wings and hops up and down without actually taking off.

The owls often squabble over food. Buffy clutches a mouse in one foot. She hisses and spreads her wings to protect her prey.

Now nearly grown, all the owls are the same size. Humpty has caught up with Buffy. It is hard to tell which sister is which.

Six months old

The owls have all flown from the hay barn. They hunt for themselves now. Buffy flies silently over the fields at night, like a huge white moth. She watches and listens for wild mice feeding and scampering in the grass below.

Other barn owls are also around. Tyto screeches as he flies. Buffy and Tyto meet. They like each other and become a pair.

One year old

Tyto and Buffy have a growing family of their own. When the owlets are tiny and pink, Buffy sits on them all the time to keep them warm. Tyto hunts and brings the food to Buffy. She pulls off tiny shreds of meat and touches her babies' beaks so they take the morsels from her. When the owlets are large and downy, she leaves them briefly to help Tyto hunt. They will need to bring hundreds of mice to the nest before the owlets are grown-up and ready to hunt for themselves.

Fun Facts About Barn Owls

1. Scientists have identified about 525 various kinds of owls.

2. Barn owls nest in old and abandoned barns and buildings. They aid farmers by helping to keep farms free of rats and mice.

3. There are ten species of barn owls. They live in most places except the colder regions.

4. The North American Barn Owl is about 18 inches (46 cm) long. Sometimes this owl is called the *Monkey-faced Owl* because its heart-shaped face, beady eyes, and amusing actions make it look like a monkey.

5. The call of a barn owl is like a weird, hissing scream.

6. The barn owl spends each night looking, listening, and hunting for mice.

7. The lives of barn owls, like those of most other owls, revolve around their territories, which are carefully chosen and marked.

8. In courtship rituals, barn owls may rub each other's cheeks or clack their bills together.

9. Barn owl hens usually lay six white eggs at one time.

10. The defense display of the barn owl is to lie flat on the ground with the wings spread horizontally.

For More Information About Animal Life

Listed below are books, magazines, and videocassettes that will provide you with more interesting information about owls. Check your local library or bookstore to see if they have them or will order them for you.

Books
Bernard, the Mischievous Little Owl and the Red Whistle. Sluder (Mascot)
The Great Horned Owl. Stone (Crestwood House)
Hoots and Toots and Hairy Brutes: *Squib the Owl Saves the Day.* Shles (Houghton Mifflin)
The Man Who Could Call Down Owls. Bunting (Macmillan)
Oolik: The Owl Who Couldn't Whoo. Jones (Glacier)
Owl at Home. Lobel (Harper & Row Jr.)
The Owl Book. Storms (Lerner)
The World of Owls. Saintsing (Gareth Stevens)
A Year in the Life of an Owl. Stidworthy (Silver Burdett)

Magazines

Chickadee
Young Naturalist Foundation
P.O. Box 11314
Des Moines, IA 50340

Owl
Young Naturalist Foundation
P.O. Box 11314
Des Moines, IA 50340

National Geographic World
National Geographic Society
P.O. Box 2330
Washington, DC 20013-9865

Ranger Rick
National Wildlife Federation
8925 Leesburg Pike
Vienna, VA 22184-0001

Videocassettes
The Barn Owl. Encyclopedia Britannica Educational Corporation, 1983.
The Owl and the Lemming. ACI Productions, 1973.

Things to Do

1. Draw three pictures of a barn owl — as a baby, an owlet, and a full-grown owl. Try to show in each picture the differences that appear in each growth stage. Then name your barn owl!

2. Try to arrange with your parents or teacher a visit to a nearby farm that has barn owls. See if you can get a photograph of one or hear some of the sounds they make.

3. Plan a trip to the zoo to look at the owls in particular (although you'll want to see the other animals, too!). Concentrate especially on the full-grown owls, the predators. Do they look fierce? Describe those aspects of the owls that make them look dangerous.

4. Go to the library and check out a good picture book on owls of all types. What are some of the most interesting differences between the various types? What are some of the characteristics that various owls have in common?

5. Owls are wily birds of prey. Make a list of some of the different animals they hunt to eat. Why are predators such as owls good to have around us? What is the particular value of predators such as the barn owl? Make a list of the good things a barn owl can do.

Things to Talk About

1. When Buffy the barn owl is born, she is "pink and blind and helpless" for quite a while. How is this similar to the condition of human babies when they are first born?

2. When food is presented to Buffy in tweezers, she immediately opens her mouth to eat. Does it seem to matter that she does not know who is feeding her? Why or why not?

3. When Buffy is very full after eating a large meal, she needs to stay quiet in order to let her food digest. What does this mean?

4. Does eating too much at one time sometimes make you sleepy? If so, why do you think this happens?

5. As Buffy and her sisters grow into owlets, they still look cute, but they are not pets. They will grow into dangerous birds of prey. What exactly does this mean? Can you think of any other animals who look cute and innocent but can be dangerous?

6. Sometimes the little owls fight over a piece of food. What kinds of things do human brothers and sisters fight over with each other?

7. As the owls grow, they learn to take care of themselves. They do not need help from each other. In what way is this true of human children?

8. As Buffy goes out on her own and finds a mate, she eventually has babies of her own. She takes care of them and teaches them in the same way her mother taught her. How is this similar to the way humans behave with their young?

Glossary of New Words

beak: a bird's bill, especially the hard bill of a bird of prey

bird of prey: a bird that feeds upon mammals and other birds, which it catches and kills

clamor: to make a loud cry in demand for something

clutch: to grasp or seize; to grip

dainty: very delicate or fragile

down: the soft, fine feathers of young birds

hatch: the successful effort of a baby animal to break free from its egg

incubator: an artificially heated area, space, or container used for hatching eggs

morsel: a small piece or amount; a tiny bit of food

pellet: a ball of undigestible matter that is periodically spit up by some animals

prey: an animal that is hunted or killed for food by another animal

scramble: to climb, scuffle, or struggle quickly for something

shred: a very small piece or fragment; to shred is also to tear something into tiny pieces

shuffle: to move around by dragging or scraping the feet

squabble: a noisy quarrel about something that is usually not very important

Index